gardenstyle
projects

Better Homes and Gardens® Books • Des Moines, Iowa

Table of contents

Better Homes and Gardens® Books, An imprint of Meredith® Books

Garden Style Projects

Editor: Linda Hallam
Senior Associate Design Director: Richard Michels
Illustrator: Lainé Roundy
Contributing Editor: Mary Baskin
Stylists/Project Designers: Patricia Mohr Kramer, Wade Scherrer
Contributing Photographers: King Au/Studio Au, Jenifer Jordan
Copy Chief: Catherine Hamrick
Copy and Production Editor: Terri Fredrickson
Contributing Copy Editor: Jay Lamar
Contributing Proofreaders: Becky Danley, Diane Doro, Margaret Smith
Indexer: Kathleen Poole
Electronic Production Coordinator: Paula Forest

Editorial and Design Assistants: Kaye Chabot, Mary Lee Gavin, Karen Schirm
Production Director: Douglas M. Johnston
Book Production Managers: Pam Kvitne, Marjorie J. Schenkelberg

Meredith® Books
Editor in Chief: James D. Blume
Design Director: Matt Strelecki
Managing Editor: Gregory H. Kayko
Executive Shelter Editor: Denise L. Caringer

Director, Sales & Marketing, Retail: Michael A. Peterson
Director, Sales & Marketing, Special Markets: Rita McMullen
Director, Sales & Marketing, Home & Garden Center Channel: Ray Wolf
Director, Operations: George A. Susral

Vice President, General Manager: Jamie L. Martin

Better Homes and Gardens® Magazine
Editor in Chief: Jean LemMon
Executive Interior Design Editor: Sandra S. Soria

Meredith Publishing Group
President, Publishing Group: Christopher M. Little
Vice President, Consumer Marketing & Development: Hal Oringer

Meredith Corporation
Chairman and Chief Executive Officer: William T. Kerr

Chairman of the Executive Committee: E. T. Meredith III

All of us at Better Homes and Gardens® Books are dedicated to providing
you with information and ideas to enhance your home. We welcome your
comments and suggestions. Write to us at: Better Homes and Gardens Books,
Shelter Editorial Department, 1716 Locust St., Des Moines, IA 50309-3023.

If you would like to purchase any of our books, check wherever quality books
are sold. Visit our website at bhg.com or bhgbooks.com.

Cover Photograph: Jenifer Jordan.

intro

Planting the style

Gardening inspires you to slow down, unwind, and take time to enjoy fresh air and sunshine. In late winter, I watch for crocuses and the first bulbs of spring to push up through the snow. By April, I'm impatient to plant my summer bulbs, annuals, and vegetables. And when the plants are in the black soil, I inspect them each day after work, looking for growth, watering when we miss a day or two of spring or summer showers. For all of us who love to garden or simply enjoy being outside, garden-style decorating erases the lines between the seasons, between indoors and out. A painted metal chair adds charm to the garden. Wouldn't a gently aged framed window leaning against the fence or a watering can in a bed of flowers be just as appealing? When your porch or deck is your favorite room, a rocking chair is naturally more comfortable with a pillow or two, along with a handy table for drinks or books. Wouldn't you enjoy your porch even more if you hung an airy fabric to block late-afternoon sun or a less-than-private view? Decorating my porch in such a simple way is how garden-style decorating started for me, and perhaps for

you too. But at the end of my first summer of relaxing on my porch-as-outdoor-room, I didn't want to give up its pleasures. So in gradual steps, the fern prints and tables and watering cans migrated into my house and through almost every room. • **As I visit garden-style decorators** around the country, I notice the creative, stylish ways they incorporate garden elements and vintage furnishings, re-purpose all manner of furniture and finds, and craft stylish art and accessories. When you decorate in this friendly style, imagination, not budget, is the key to a pretty, inviting home. Need a plant stand? What could be better than an old ladder with discreetly peeling paint? Want extra seating in the dining room? Add a padded seat to a metal garden bench. Tired of dark, mismatched furniture? Paint it white or pale pink or yellow and add floral decals. No headboard for your bed or art above the mantel? Look for shutters, windows, doors, gates. Need an extra bedside table? Introduce a folding wooden or metal chair and stack gardening books to a comfortable height. Or buy a reproduction or vintage folding, slatted, wooden patio table and re-purpose it as a handy bedside accessory. • **For lighthearted accents** for their homes, garden-style decorators adapt as well as re-purpose outdoor pieces. For example, with a well-crafted, stable base, almost any outdoor object transforms into a functional, decorative table. Columns and oversized brackets are possibilities for one-of-a-kind table bases. Columns, cut to fit, are handsome as floor lamps and as plant stands. Tools take on new uses in garden style. One of my favorite examples is a ladder hung horizontally to decoratively display quilts (pages 84-85). • **Another favorite project** involves both decorating and crafting. Two friends, Wade Scherrer and Patty Kramer, helped me decorate the guest room in my house (pages 58-59). Wade suggested the green and white scheme. Patty designed and painted the fern-pattern screen that substitutes for a headboard and the leaf motifs on white bed linens. She created the memory boxes with herbs from her garden. Wade found an inexpensive white chandelier from a home center and a discount store table skirt, both with leaf motifs. This combination of serendipitous finds and nature-inspired crafts is the theme of *Garden Style Projects*. Many other garden-style decorators around the country shared their ideas and projects and entertaining schemes. Step-by-step instructions and alternative ideas are included. For every room of your home, you'll find inspiration for collecting, arranging, and re-purposing, as well as directions for projects that turn ordinary materials into furnishings and accessories. Relax and enjoy a stylish way of living, decorating, and entertaining. That's what garden style is about.

Linda Hallam, Editor, Garden Style Projects

Fresh-air living

Start your own fresh-air decorating where outdoor style begins—in your garden or on your porch, terrace, or deck. In these easy-living spaces, the simplest touches create the look and feel of a comfortable living area. Decorate your porch with trellises, thrift store art, a collection of straw hats. Or liven up a plain deck with decorative shutters or old garden tools. Add cushions to make porch chairs more comfortable and include tables for lamps, drinks, and magazines. Such carefree pleasures are the essence of this friendly style. When you are ready to furnish your fresh-air living room, think about re-purposing everyday objects. Pair a patio table with old wooden folding chairs, painted for casual dining. Fill a wood ladder or child's wagon with plants. Plant vintage watering cans with seasonal flowers and ivy. Dress up a porch floor with a painted floorcloth or casual sisal rug. Shade a sunny porch corner with gently draped cotton fabric. When you dine outside, dress your table with one or, better yet, two colorful tablecloths. If you are in the mood for a project, stencil a garden motif on a plain tablecloth or napkins.

Privacy for porch dining

Porch living defines the relaxed essence of garden style. But if your porch gets too much sun or faces neighbors or a busy street, use easy-to-sew drapery panels to create a feeling of seclusion. Close the draperies as needed or pull them back to frame the garden view. For the romance of outdoor dining, hang a candle chandelier above your table and chairs. Look for vintage chandeliers in shops that specialize in garden antiques. Reproduction candle chandeliers are also available through garden-style and home decorating catalogs.

◀ **1.** Buy bamboo poles at a garden shop or nursery. For a wide opening, measure and cut poles to fit and connect ends over a dowel rod. Install the bamboo pole with closet rod holders. Hang a bracket support to prevent unsightly sagging.

▶ **2.** Purchase cotton print drapery fabric or a lightweight canvas. Sew draperies as flat panels with 3-inch pockets at the top. Sew matching tie-backs. Or, if you prefer, purchase similar drapery panels in a style compatible with your porch.

▶ **3.** Slip a bungee cord through each tie-back and anchor it to the porch column with a small hook. This allows for give when the wind blows. As an alternative for a rustic-style porch, substitute twine for fabric tie-backs. Ribbon also works for a dressier look.

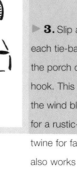

Create an oasis of calm

turn to the serenity of an Oriental garden as inspiration for a quiet sitting area. Start with a painted floorcloth you make by painting the back side of a vinyl remnant from a home center. The vinyl gives a durable surface that withstands fading on a porch. Paint a natural shade of tan for the look of a woven rug. If you are reviving old wicker, paint with the same shade of warm tan. Before painting wicker, brush off flaking paint, wash it with mild soap and water, and rinse well. Allow wicker pieces to dry before repainting.

1. Prime. Apply exterior latex. Dry. Draw a grid of 1-foot squares. Tape off every other square in first row. Skip a row; repeat taping. For a comb, cut ¼-inch notches from squeegee. Brush tan paint in the first square. Pull comb through the square.

2. Wipe paint from the comb. Repeat the same technique to form a checkerboard pattern. At the first row, tape off uncombed squares. Work in smooth, even motions with a firm stroke. (Practice first on scrap to be confident of the look you want.)

3. Apply paint; pull comb at a right angle to previous combing direction. Drag comb through paint again, across the lines just combed. Wipe the comb after every drag to avoid paint accumulating in the notches.

4. Immediately place the comb in original position and pull through paint in zigzag motion. This makes a herringbone pattern. Remove tape. Repeat technique for unpainted squares. Allow to dry. Seal with two coats of satin-finish polyurethane.

Relax white with soft pastels

▶ Contrast rough textures and whites as backgrounds for floral-filled rooms or simple garden houses. Distressed finishes and worn iron nicely balance delicate floral fabrics and soft cushions. And mixed bouquets, in salvaged containers, recall the charm of flowers picked on country walks. Framed art stands out in such a relaxed, fresh ambience.

◄ Introduce pink in whimsical, unexpected ways. For this porch, the owner painted a decorative window box in her favorite light tint and accented with a pink watering can and maple syrup bucket. To perk up the rocking chair's throw pillow, she tied on two sheer, floral scarves.

Classic white takes on an appealing, youthful charm with touches of pink and floral accents. Spruce up your small porch or garden house with a fresh coat of white paint. Update your furnishings, too, with this clean, summer cottage look. Introduce shades of pink as lighthearted, surprising accents. Enrich with woven textures and time-worn, peeling metal finishes.

Metal yard chairs

Once known as motel chairs, brightly enameled metal armchairs embraced the industrial, mass production designs of the 1930s and 1940s. The affordable and durable chairs graced front porches and backyards until the advent of folding mesh and plastic chairs in the 1960s. Relegated to secondhand shops, garage sales, and

trash heaps for 30 years, these chairs have regained their popularity as American icons. Enthusiasts scour flea markets and yard sales for the original chairs for picturesque interior accents as well as for sturdy porch and deck furniture. Mass merchandisers note the appeal, and metal chairs again offer affordable style.

The deck as outdoor room

1. Purchase two colors of semitransparent deck stain. Wash the deck according to directions on can. Determine size of rug and location. Mark a corner with a T square and chalk. Pull a chalk line to establish the first side. Repeat for each side.

2. For a border, make four chalk lines inside the outline. Mark off the diamonds in your determined size. Diagonally connect guide points with a chalk line to create diamond shapes. Score lines with a utility knife to prevent stain from bleeding.

3. Beginning at the center, stain every other diamond with the lighter stain. Use a disposable sponge applicator for straight edges; fill in with a tapered bristle brush. Let dry. Stain remaining diamonds and border with darker-color stain.

d ress your deck the easy way with salvaged louvered shutters for sun control or privacy. Hinge together two or three full-length shutters. For more instant style, look for old paneled doors, with the hardware intact, that can casually lean against your house. Don't worry about matching doors—a mix of finishes and paint colors increases the allure. Give your decking its own checkerboard rug (directions above) for your collection of outdoor furniture. If you enjoy the twig look, add colorful pillows for relaxed comfort.

Energize with patterns

Call on the power of color to enliven your porch or patio. Consider a standard, suburban porch with a poured concrete floor as a neutral starting point to your ideas and creativity. Just as garden plantings are beautiful in a range of palettes from the palest to the most intense, so too is your garden style. Here, a decorative painter used her favorite vibrant colors and lively, stylized floral motifs to infuse the porch with a tropical ambience. When she finished the floor, she painted, then planted, a collection of cheerful terra-cotta pots.

▶ **1.** Clean the concrete floor with water. Allow to dry. Apply concrete cleaner and etcher per directions on can. Choose two colors of concrete stain (water reducible acrylic). Roll on the lightest color. Repeat base coat.

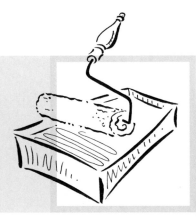

▶ **2.** Determine the size of the diamonds and how they will be placed on the floor. Measure with a yardstick and mark width and length points. Draw in diamonds, with a straightedge and pencil, by matching the marked points.

▶ **3.** Tape to the outside or inside of each diamond. Paint the darker color inside the diamond. Repeat if color is uneven. Allow paint to dry 72 hours; pull off tape. Wait 30 days for the paint to set before placing furniture or heavy pots on the porch.

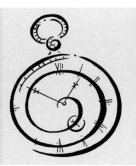

Perk up with polka dots

1. Cut prewashed fabric into the desired cushion shape. Mix acrylic yellow paint with textile medium, following directions on the medium bottle. Stir well. Brush paint on the fabric so it seeps through to the underside. Allow fabric to dry thoroughly.

◀ **2.** With circle template, draw random polka dots over the fabric. Cover the fabric in an overall pattern for the most interesting look. Mix your polka-dot accent colors with acrylic medium. Stir before painting as mixed paint tends to separate.

◀ **3.** With a ¾-inch brush, fill in outlined polka dots with the crafts paint mixture. Allow to dry. Outline each polka dot with a gold fabric pen. Air dry for 24 hours. Heat-set according to directions on the medium bottle. Sew pillows as desired.

energize your porch, deck, or patio with the instant—and economical—power of paint. As these projects show, easy techniques transform everyday objects, such as plastic window planters and pots, and cotton fabric, into lively accessories. Choose lively colors that work with the exterior paint scheme of your house and landscape. Outdoor spaces get sun exposure, especially in the summer when they are most in use, so you can use brighter colors than you might think. Temper with terra-cotta and cool white.

1. Wipe plastic with denatured alcohol. Spray with acrylic burnt sienna paint. Evenly apply self-adhesive office labels. With a pencil and ruler, draw diamonds. Run ¼-inch tape along edges of stickers.

2. For a bright, but not overpowering color for your planter, mix three parts of yellow enamel with one part white enamel paint. Stir well. Apply the paint with ¾-inch brush over the stickers and tape for smooth, even coverage.

3. Outline the diamonds with a small artist's brush and fill in with the yellow paint mixture. Allow to dry. If necessary for coverage, apply a second coat. Allow to dry completely. Vibrant French blue or green also work well as porch accent colors.

4. Use a safety-edge razor to cut along edges of tape and stickers. Remove tape, then stickers. Outline edges with a gold paint pen. Spray with two coats of clear sealant. Allow drying between coats. Wait 24 hours before planting.

finding
& displaying

Tool and container art

in the spirit of garden style, choose portable containers to plant with a mix of perennials and

seasonal blooming plants. Collect a variety of containers—from modest clay pots to

decorative urns to cast pieces—to fill with color throughout the year. The containers, paired

with small tables and old gardening tools, move with the seasons, from indoors to out and

Textures from nature

Relax your fresh-air setting with the soothing colors and materials of the outdoors. You'll create an environment that invites slowing down and taking the time to enjoy the pleasures of garden style. Natural wood and fibers and dried seasonal flowers all contribute in their own ways to a serene, back-to-the-earth decorating scheme. The secret? Choose the elements with care and strive for simplicity. You'll be rewarded with a quiet oasis amid the busy swirls of your modern life.

◄ Hang a drying rack on your porch wall as both a practical and a decorative element. Add collected vintage tools, drying flower blooms, and a straw hat or two. A wicker porch swing, made all the more comfortable with a mix of floral cushions, entices you to afternoons of carefree reading and napping.

► Dress up a garden house or potting shed the simplest way possible with a bamboo trellis from the nursery for fast-climbing, blooming vines. Fill a window box with moss and seasonal flowers that casually climb over your windows. You'll transform a utilitarian space into an appealing focal point.

Make your own fountain

◄ **1.** Have an electrician install an outdoor electrical outlet with ground fault circuit interrupter. Buy a submersible pump and a pot at least 30 inches in diameter from a nursery or home center. Pull the pump's electrical cord through the drainage hole.

◄ **2.** After the cord is pulled through, seal the hole in the pot with a quick-drying cement compound. Allow the cement to dry thoroughly. Save this outside job for warm, dry weather for best results and fastest drying. Choose a plain or decorative clay pot.

► **3.** Seal the inside with liquid water sealant. Allow to dry. Elevate the pump on stacked bricks until it is a few inches below the water line. Fill with water to desired level. Follow manufacturer's directions for installing the pump.

nwind to the soft sounds of a bubbling fountain. Water, the ultimate source of life, soothes and cools in any setting. If you live in the city or on a busy street, gurgling water masks the noises of daily life—a definite plus in enjoying your outdoor retreat. Plant lush annuals around your fountain to complete the idyllic setting. One note of caution: water attracts mosquitoes. Stock your fountain in summer with small goldfish that eat the hatching larvae. Or purchase a chemical ring, safe for birds or goldfish, from a nursery.

1. Dig a ground trench sized to fit salvaged grinding stones. One end should be lower to hold water plants and to conceal the pump. See the pump directions and additional information on the opposite page.

2. Line the fountain reservoir with a rubber pond liner. Outline the reservoir with brick or stone. Make sure the liner is above the anticipated water line. Place several spacers on the floor of the reservoir.

3. Stack three grinding stones, with tubing through the centers, on top of the spacers. Place a gasket in the top stone for a snug fit. Level stones. Cover floor with stones. Add water. Turn on the pump and relax.

Worn watering cans

ike much in the history of gardening, watering cans came into their own in the Victorian era. In the late 19th century, the middle class discovered gardening as a fashionable hobby. Tools and well-designed, functional watering cans abounded, not only in the British Isles but throughout Europe and across the United States

as well. These prewar European watering cans are sold in fashionable shops that specialize in gardening antiques. Easy to find at flea markets and secondhand shops are painted and plain-metal, American watering cans made from the 1930s through the 1950s. Funky versions, crafted from metal cans, are highly prized as folk art.

Dress your deck for supper

Choose a theme and a color scheme to ready your deck for warm-weather living and entertaining. What could be more natural for a gardener than watering cans and shades of green? Plant a can or two with summer annuals and vines. Repeat the motif for a stenciled green tablecloth that skirts an outdoor patio table. (See page 165 for the pattern and directions.) Pair with several vintage wood folding chairs. For a final touch, stripe a plain plank deck with two shades of opaque stain, compatible with your siding color.

◄ 1. See pattern and stencil directions on page 164. Photo copy the design or resize to the desired scale you choose for your tablecloth, runner, or napkins. Tape the design to stencil plastic and trace with a fine marker or felt tip pen.

◄ 2. Cut out the design with a crafts knife. Work on a self-healing cutting mat, available at art supply stores, or on a surface you don't mind scratching. Cut out paper watering cans and pin to your tablecloth to help you place your stenciled motifs.

▶ 3. Practice on a scrap. After the design is cut out, tape to your smooth, ironed fabric with stencil tape, less tacky than regular tape. Apply stencil paint with a stencil brush. Move firmly in a circular motion. Untape and pull off stencil in a quick motion.

chapter two

The garden inside

Garden style transcends the season when you decorate with the ornaments and elements of the outdoors. For this most personal of styles, think about what you enjoy about nature and the garden. Decorate easily and casually in the relaxed spirit of the outdoors with projects that are fast and fun. What could be quicker than filling your firebox in summer with a collection of clay pots? Arrange others on the mantel and the hot-weather look is complete. For style at the hearth, elevate houseplants on stools or bamboo stands. Replace a standard interior door with a charming, old-fashioned screen door when privacy isn't an issue. The list extends as far as your imagination. In winter, bring the garden inside with fresh colors, wall treatments, fabrics, and plants. Paint a bedroom wall with freehand flowers and hang framed, pressed flowers from your summer garden. Use a clever painting technique for a fern screen (pages 58 and 59) that instantly turns a corner into a woodland-style oasis. When you fill your home with the green of the garden, you'll relax and unwind in a fragrant, plant-filled retreat on even the bleakest winter days.

Stencil dragonfly motifs

easy projects transform a traditional dining room into year-round summer. Linen sheets trimmed with cream banding inspire the sophisticated neutral scheme. Recycle pillowcases into chair-back slip-covers; cut and hem the fitted bottom sheet for the seat covers. Save the banded top sheet for the table runner. Detail linens with a stencil from a dragonfly pattern; see page 164 for pattern and directions. For a luncheon, hang straw hats from the chandelier and on the wall. To be safe, keep the lights turned off.

◄ 1. Slip a pillowcase over a chair back and measure how far slits need to be cut to fit properly. Open the side seams of the pillowcase and hem back with a narrow hem. For seat covers, cut rectangles from a fitted sheet, hem, and lay over seats.

◄ 2. Make the stencil with stencil plastic from a crafts store (see pages 34, 35, and 164). Cut out paper patterns of your stencil motifs; place on fabric for spacing. Replace with stencil and apply paint with pouncing motion.

► 3. Hold the stencil firmly in place. Fill in the edges of the stencil, going over any blank spaces. Pull back the stencil, being careful not to smear paint. Allow to dry to avoid smudges. Follow manufacturer's directions on the fabric for laundering.

Prints and patterns

transform neutral rooms and plain furnishings into instant garden style when you introduce

prints, art, and touches of patterned fabric. Identically framed vintage or reproduction prints

create a focal point in a neutral room. Repeat with touches of patterned fabrics to unify your

delicate floral scheme. Consider pale, soft backgrounds and painted white furniture as back-

drops for your ever-changing displays of collections and seasonal flowers from the garden.

Tie on summery slipcovers

restyle your dining room into a sophisticated European pavilion with moss green walls, found objects, and simple-to-sew slipcovers. A pair of columns and a decorative fragment from an architectural salvage house stand out against the repainted walls and uncovered windows. To relax standard dining chairs into the garden look, sew one-piece cotton slipcovers that have the charm of a summer dress. Mix with floral upholstered chairs and a flat-woven kilim rug for touches of color and pattern. A French-style iron chandelier and sturdy pine farm table complete the look of alfresco dining.

◀ **1.** For fabric yardage for solids, measure from the bottom of the back over the top to the floor in front. Add an extra inch on four sides. Measure from floor to seat, add an inch; double. Add the two measurements together.

▶ **2.** Cut the body and side pieces of the slipcover from your length of fabric. Stitch together on the wrong side with a 1-inch seam. Hem the remaining edges with a ½-inch doubled hem.

▶ **3.** Fold and stitch ties sewn from extra fabric. Place the one-piece slipcover on the chair and pin the ties for the correct position. Hand stitch in place. (If you are matching plaid or repeats, you'll need extra fabric.)

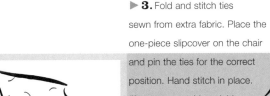

◄ Paint or wallpaper your dining room walls in lighthearted stripes. Update an old chest and mirror frame with palest pink paint. Lightly distress the chest by randomly rubbing with sandpaper to emulate the look of natural wear. For a floral finishing touch, apply a decal bouquet from a crafts store.

Introduce stripes and checks

pair your favorite floral designs with crisp stripes or jaunty checks for dining rooms that feel fresh, not fussy. The all-pink dining room (above) takes on the mood of a seaside cottage pavilion with hand-painted striped walls and a painted chest detailed with a floral decal. In the dining room (at right) florals mix with picnic-cloth checks. Primary colors and easy-care fabrics impart a friendly feel to rooms where the family gathers.

► Collect vintage and new fabrics that work in your personal decorating scheme. Here, red, repeated in the floral Roman shades and slipcovers, ties the look together. Revive old kitchen chairs with casual slipcovers. Add quick-sew pillows for pattern and relaxed comfort. Layer a floral cloth over checks.

Paint an indoor trellis

1. Choose your brush width for the dimensions of the trellis. A 3-inch brush works well. Brush horizontal, then vertical lines. Allow the trellis to dry. With a tapered artist's brush, outline and fill in the roses and leaves with white crafts paint.

2. If you want to alter or enlarge shapes, reoutline. The charm is in the painterly look. Paint in roses and leaves. Use a medium green crafts paint for the leaves and your choice of pink or another pastel for the roses.

3. With a small artist's brush, start on the outside edges and detail roses with darker crafts paint. Mix dark paint with the background color of the roses and paint another swirl. Outline the leaves with dark green crafts paint; paint details as shown.

Savor spring flowers every day of the year with an easy-to-paint trellis decorated with charmingly stylized roses and leaves. Add the trellis below the chair rail in your garden-style living, dining, or breakfast room. Also consider the technique for a focal-point wall or for settings such as a small powder room, nursery, or child's room. Or, paint your walls a pretty apple green, sky blue, or shell pink and add a crisp white trellis twined with delicate yellow roses. Without measuring or taping, paint the horizontal lines for the easy trellis. Drag down the vertical lines to complete.

finding
&
displaying

Add elements of age

decorate your rooms with the textures of vintage pieces from garden-style antiques stores and flea markets. Mix your favorite furnishings, fragments, and finds from nature to create rooms that are easy to live in and change with the seasons. Keep the backgrounds neutral to avoid

Picnic in the garden

enjoy your living room even more with wallpaper, fabrics, furnishings, and finishing touches that recall an impromptu picnic in the flower garden. For a garden-style living room, the botanical wallpaper sets the backdrop for old-fashioned floral fabrics and collected, distressed tables. A ladder displays the houseplants that contribute to the always-springtime style. As a special touch, the owner hung her favorite vintage cotton picnic cloths, collected from flea markets and antiques fairs, from salvaged architectural brackets.

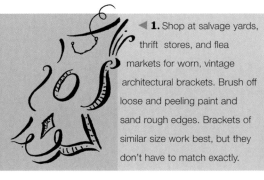

◄ 1. Shop at salvage yards, thrift stores, and flea markets for worn, vintage architectural brackets. Brush off loose and peeling paint and sand rough edges. Brackets of similar size work best, but they don't have to match exactly.

► 2. Attach brackets to the wall with hangers designed for framed art. Purchase hardware according to the weight of the bracket. (If you need more picnic cloths than you can find, use an old one as a sewing pattern.)

3. Alternative hanging: drill holes in the brackets to hang. Knot cloths to the brackets as shown. Or loosely knot the picnic cloths and tack in place with clear pushpins. Tack from the underside of the knots.

Warm with textures

◀ Organize a kitchen or breakfast room display with a bamboo pole as a drying rack. Add hooks as needed to hang baskets and to suspend dried flowers and fall sheaths. A twig rack for tea towels and a sturdy bench, styled with cheerful fabrics, contribute to the autumn-garden ambience for dining.

invite nature into your home with the relaxed neutrals and comforting textures of country gardens and woodlands. For stress-free rooms, mix light woods, such as natural pine, with sisal rugs, bamboo, gently worn finishes, baskets, and dried flowers. Choose floral fabrics with tea-stained backgrounds or soft, grayed colors for harmonious touches. Accent with carefully arranged, vintage-style art and botanical accessories.

▶ Channel your collecting into edited and grouped arrangements that make the most of your finds. For visual anchors to your collections, search markets for matched sets, such as the stacked hat boxes, and for pairs, such as the round tole trays. Orderly arrangements allow each piece to be appreciated.

Blossoming floral patterns

name your favorite flower, and chances are you'll find a fabric, wallpaper, or piece of pottery or porcelain in an appealing motif. In the realm of collecting, garden devotees are rediscovering English chintzware, decorated porcelains and pottery that emulate the well-known floral fabric. The pretty, tightly detailed porcelain

designs, manufactured and exported from the late 1920s through the early 1950s, transformed tea sets, bowls, vases, and small clocks into art. If your inclination is to the casual, look for floral patterns in handkerchiefs, pottery, enamelware, and metal trays. The affordable colletibles are easy to find at thrift shops and flea markets.

Garden gate dreams

decorate your daughter's room with a garden theme that's pretty—but not quickly outgrown. For this spunky space, the mother and daughter team started with an old-fashioned floral bouquet wallpaper that sets the blue, pink, and white palette. Handmade picket-fence beds and white woodwork, including salvaged brackets, ensure the mood stays light and young. For finishing summer garden touches, the decorators shopped for the metal chair, painted ladder, maple syrup buckets, and the watering can that stores art supplies.

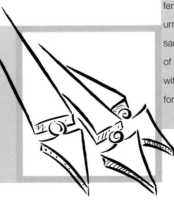

▶ **1.** Purchase standard twin metal bed frames. Purchase unfinished porch or newel posts, finials, pickets, and four 2x4s, cut to fit, for each bed. For more picket detailing, have a millwork shop cut decorative pickets.

2. To emulate the look of garden fencing, prime and paint unfinished wood. (If you prefer, sand rough spots.) For the look of whitewashing, dilute the paint with water. Nail pickets to 2x4s for headboards as shown.

▶ **3.** For footboard, turn the top 2x4 horizontally and rest on the pickets as shown. Glue in place with wood glue. Glue finials in place with clear wood glue. Sand off dried, excess glue. Attach head and footboard to frame with screws to complete.

Paint a woodland setting

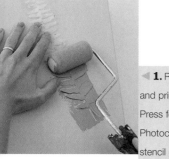

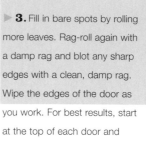

1. Remove door hinges, sand, and prime. Apply base paint. Press four to six leaves. Photocopy leaves and trace onto stencil plastic. Cut out. Mix glaze as a 1-to-1 ratio of paint to neutral glaze. Place leaf shapes on door and glaze with roller.

◀**2.** Reverse-stencil one section of each door at a time. Fill in and vary the angles and shapes of the leaves for a pleasing effect. Leaves can overlap slightly, and several can be rolled at once. Rag-roll over stenciled leaves with a damp rag to blend colors.

▶**3.** Fill in bare spots by rolling more leaves. Rag-roll again with a damp rag and blot any sharp edges with a clean, damp rag. Wipe the edges of the door as you work. For best results, start at the top of each door and work in 2-foot sections.

turn your bedroom into a verdant oasis with a serene green-and-white scheme. Choose green, the color with the power to soothe and calm, as the backdrop for freshly painted walls. Repeat in varying shades as the accents for a painted screen, made from bifold doors, and the leaf-detailed all-cotton linens. To complete your room redo, skirt a table with a readymade cloth and add a natural cotton coverlet and woven rug. Edit accessories to the minimum and include leaf-decorated boxes for stylish bedside storage.

1. Practice drawing on scrap paper. With a soft lead pencil, draw the first leaf 3 inches from sheet edge. Space leaves 1½ inches apart. Allow a 3-inch border. Draw in S-shape line between leaves.

▶ **2.** Hand-paint the leaf outlines with a small artist's detail brush. Use crafts paint in a shade of green. Add a vein down the center of each leaf. Sheets can be washed and dried when the paint is dry.

  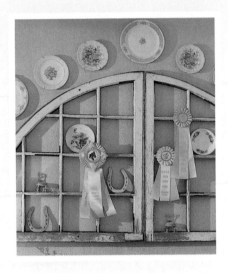

Country inn guest room

Welcome your company to spring in the country with a guest room that boasts the style and

comforts of a charming inn. Include your favorite floral fabrics, plenty of pillows, and a cud-

dly floral chenille bedspread. Bring in a pair of cushioned wicker armchairs with a lamp for

A porch for boys' play

Picture the friendly porches of western ranch houses to create a boy-pleasing bedroom. A pair of shutters, a vintage door, and flags give the room its parade-day ambience while a sturdy, flat-woven kilim rug and lodge-style linens spark the primary color scheme. What could hold up better in such an active play space than an aged, painted Adirondack chair from the secondhand store and a garden bench turned into the repository for boots? Old egg baskets, from a neighborhood flea market, organize books and magazines.

1. Add character to a room with a vintage door. To clean the door, brush off dirt and loose paint. Scrub flaking paint chips with a brush dipped in sudsy water. Allow to dry. Seal the dry door with clear polyurethane.

2. To install, remove the existing door with a screwdriver. Save the hinges. If the door is small for your opening, securely nail a finishing strip to the inside of the door frame. Add decorative vintage hardware.

3. If you find a decorative door that is too large for the opening, have it planed to size and sanded at a millwork shop. Reattach original hardware to frame if removed; screw in hinges; and hang your new old door.

Washroom nostalgia

◄ When space allows, include an old-fashioned, thrift-store dressing table and mirrors in ornate picture frames. Instead of a medicine cabinet, hang open shelving for supplies. If you don't need the undersink storage provided by a built-in cabinet, paint the base and pipe in your favorite garden hue.

▶ Re-purpose your finds to outfit your bath. Who needs towel racks when an old wire bin, a wonderfully aged ladder, and robe hooks can be pressed into service? Doesn't an old side chair, painted palest pink, serve quite nicely as a table? Add the flourishes of a needlepoint rug and art.

WILLS'S WOODBINES

greet the morning with the pleasures of the outdoors when you decorate a bath with fresh colors and vintage finds. Touches that evoke the baths of summer cottages count for more than high-tech conveniences. Keep the feel clean and uncluttered with pale paint colors and quick storage for your bath essentials. Animate with accent colors and florals for spirited contrast.

Blooms in the boudoir

express your decorating creativity with painted wall motifs—and pressed flowers from your garden. Here, flowers from an early summer garden set the color mood for a bedroom in warm yellows, accented by cooler touches of blue and purple. In keeping with the simplicity of the room, pressed flowers are displayed in natural-wood frames with a precut mat from a discount store. The flowers and leaf-covered boxes share cupboard space with vintage floral chenille spreads—combining the pretty with practical bedroom storage.

◄ 1. Paint walls with two coats of eggshell latex. Decide spacing of stripes. Measure and mark the top and bottom points for the stripes. With a thick artist's brush and crafts paint, handpaint stripes with breaks. Outline and paint flowers and leaves.

◄ 2. Enlarge flowers as needed to fill breaks in stripes. Allow flowers and leaves to completely dry to prevent smudging. Outline and detail flowers and leaves with a fine-line, gray felt-tip pen. This adds dimension to the bouquets.

► 3. Age the dry walls with commercial antiquing glaze from a home center or paint store. Try first in an inconspicuous corner to make sure you like this enriching effect. Lightly rub the glaze over the painted walls with clean, lint-free cotton rags.

chapter three

Furniture and finds

Outdoor furniture inside, new purposes for old pieces, finishes that gently age—all contribute to garden style. With the ever-growing interest in gardening and garden-style decorating, you'll find more and more choices in outdoor furniture. To make the most of your finds, look for pieces that are at home inside as well as on the porch and patio. Beyond new and reproduction metal and wood furniture, garden-style shops around the country are importing iron and decorative wire pieces from Europe, Mexico, and South America. You'll find patio sets of tables and chairs as well as armchairs, lounge chairs, smaller drink tables, and plant stands. Feel free to mix styles, finishes, old, and new. As long as the scale and materials are compatible, creative pairing is part of the fun. Creativity is also a big part of re-purposing garden elements or old furnishings. In this milieu, introduce simple elements—new or gently aged birdbaths topped with glass or leaded windows on sturdy bases for innovative tables. Paint chests, washstands, tables, or chairs white or pale pastels for an inexpensive and fashionable update.

Distress a painted bench

if you can't find the right aged piece for your home, distress your own previously painted or unfinished furniture. You'll have the look you love and a bench, table, or other furnishing that is sized and styled for your home. And when you distress a piece yourself, you choose the colors that work with your setting. Here, blue and red reinforce the bold palette in a room filled with an American country spirit. If you prefer a touch of the European country, consider French blue and golden yellow. Or for a springtime-in-the-garden mood, pair pale green with white or medium green with pale yellow.

◀ **1.** Sand and prime unfinished piece. If already painted, wipe with a tack cloth and paint the base color. Or prime again and then paint with the base color. Allow to dry. Rub wax over paint with the grain. Concentrate on edges and areas of natural wear.

◀ **2.** Brush on the top coat. If the bench will be used outside or on a porch, choose exterior latex paint to avoid fading. Interior latex is fine if the bench will be used primarily in a protected area. Allow the top coat to dry thoroughly before continuing.

▶ **3.** Place the bench on a drop cloth. Sand with medium-grade sandpaper until you achieve the effect. (Repeat with waxing, painting, and sanding for a third color, if desired.) Wipe bench with tack cloth and seal with two coats of polyurethane.

Introduce scrolled metal

Simplify your dining style with sturdy, metal furnishings. For a low-key, restful mood inside, choose soft neutral or pale pastel tints for walls. Look for major pieces of furniture in earthy colors and natural finishes. For the most interest, pair metal or painted pieces with natural wood or wicker. Outside, durable metal and stone furnishings are naturals for lush settings tucked into private, shady, corners of your garden or on the deck or patio.

◀ Originally designed for a porch, this decorative bench with ruffled pillows recalls the picturesque motifs of Victorian-era houses. Enjoy such a find year-round as seating for a farm-style pine dining table. Repeat the decorative metal accents with scrolled ice cream parlor chairs for the host and hostess.

▶ Re-create the mystery of a hideaway hacienda with scrolled iron chairs imported from Mexico or South America. The curves give a sensuous, sophisticated air to the setting while the openness allows the garden to star. You'll find both dark metal and painted white finishes in new and vintage pieces.

Aged finishes impart style

give your setting the benefit of experience with one wonderful furniture piece that proudly shows its age. Just one element, when it's chosen with care, sets the mood for a room. Look for sturdy tables, chests, or cabinets that have stories to tell, as they impart textures and subtle color variations. These well-made pieces have survived years of use as hardworking home furnishings. Put them to work for family meals or storage and relish your ties to the past.

Craft a column floor lamp

1 ight up your garden-style sitting area with a lamp base made from an aged porch column. If you can't find the right-sized salvaged column, purchase a new one from a lumberyard or home center and practice the gentle art of distressing. (See pages 70-71 for the technique.) With this easy start, pad a metal or wood garden bench with chenille-covered cushions and accent pillows. Include a distressed bench or a stool for a handy small table. Add floral pillows, made from fabric remnants, to a slipcovered armchair and hang favorite floral plates, prints, or finds on the wall. Your haven is complete.

◀ 1. Find a hollow porch post or column, or one that can be drilled with a long bit. Purchase a retail lamp kit from a crafts or discount store. Purchase a base or cut one from ¾-inch plywood.

2. Follow the kit directions for lamp conversions. Drop the cord through the column and through the hole drilled in the base. Attach the base with wood glue and finishing nails. The base stabilizes the column.

▶ 3. Buy a shade in scale with your lamp. Spray on two or three coats of paint in your color choice. Color-copy motifs or cut out flowers or other patterns from wallpaper. Glue to the shade with crafts glue. Allow to dry and seal with a spray fixative.

Aged and distressed finishes

time mellows the garden—and garden structures and ornaments. And the beauty of the fresh and new gently evolves into the mature plants and well-worn elements of the garden. Garden furnishings and art are valued as the seasons etch their own imprints into the simplest pieces. Just as such well-worn pieces that proudly bear

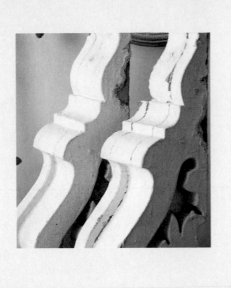

their ages enrich our gardens, so do they anchor our homes. Start small with a bracket or fragment arranged with books on a shelf or mantel. Fill a flat basket with a collection of porch spindles. As your interests evolve, scour flea markets or thrift stores for a table, chair, or bench that fits—peeling paint and all—into your home.

Refresh your work space

◀ Make a desk in a snap with the stylish and easy pairing of painted sawhorses and a ½-inch-thick tempered-glass top. (Have the edges smoothed for safety.) Search flea markets and art shows for good buys in floral still lifes and landscapes. Lean, rather than hang, so you can easily change the art.

▶ Turn to the more formal gardens of England and France for inspiration for your work space. Relax a traditional writing table and chair with a metal gate as an invitation board. Collect outdoor finds, such as vintage artist's paint boxes and garden-game balls. Save space for art pottery to fill with flowers.

Surround yourself with your favorite things—and even the chores of personal paperwork take on a more reflective mood. Little touches, from healthy houseplants and fresh flowers to candles, lanterns, garden ornaments, woven mats, and botanical art, relax daily stresses when they grace your home office. Incorporate the outdoors with practical baskets and bins for storage.

Easy-sew puffs of pillows

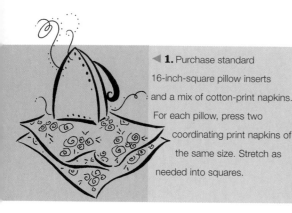

◀ **1.** Purchase standard 16-inch-square pillow inserts and a mix of cotton-print napkins. For each pillow, press two coordinating print napkins of the same size. Stretch as needed into squares.

2. Stitch the zipper to one side of each napkin. Fold napkins with wrong sides together. Topstitch the remaining three edges, following the existing hemming stitch. Insert the pillow form and zip closed.

▶ **3.** As a quick zipperless alternative, press two napkins, stretch as needed into squares, and place with right sides together. Stitch three sides and turn. Insert the pillow form. Hand-or machine-stitch the fourth side. Mix prints for an interesting look.

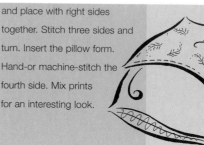

revive garden furniture with an array of pillows. On sunny days, bring the pillows outside for touches of color and comfort. With stylish cotton napkins and tea towels sold in a variety of colors and motifs, it's easy and inexpensive to sew all the pillows you desire. Mix patterns in coordinating colors for reversible pillows that add to your decorating possibilities. Beyond stripes, checks, and florals, look for bamboo and other botanical motifs. Damask-style or garden-theme tea towels cover standard, rectangular pillows.

1. Buy two matching or coordinating cotton tea towels. Look for one pattern in two different color combinations. Purchase a small rectangular travel pillow. Mark lines on the wrong side of one towel for placement of hem tape.

2. Press on hem tape. Remove paper backing and add second towel on top (wrong sides together). Press, leaving an opening for pillow. Press opening together. Spot clean, rather than launder, as the hem tape is delicate.

Ladders large and small

Support a ladder on decorative brackets—and a utilitarian object is transformed into an art-

ful rack for prized quilts. For a pleasing arrangement, fold and hang the quilts at varying lev-

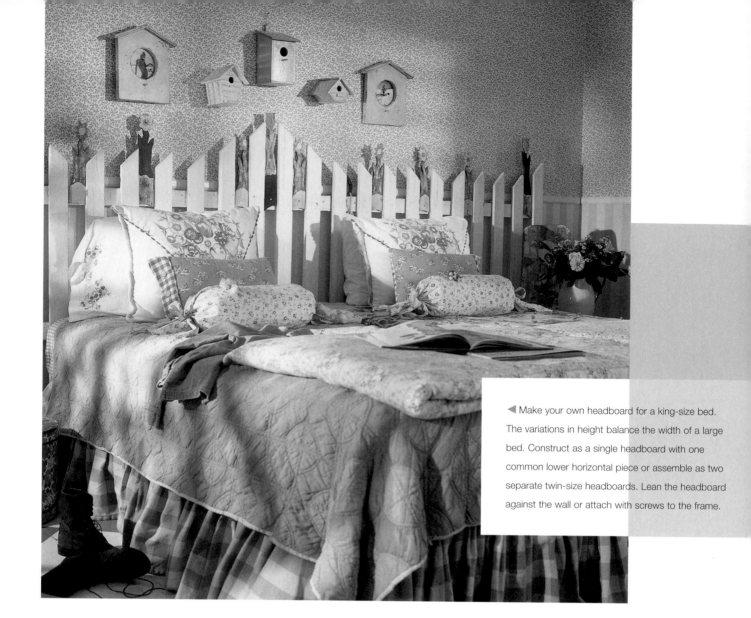

◄ Make your own headboard for a king-size bed. The variations in height balance the width of a large bed. Construct as a single headboard with one common lower horizontal piece or assemble as two separate twin-size headboards. Lean the headboard against the wall or attach with screws to the frame.

Sleeping in a flower garden

Start your bedroom decorating with the mood-setting focal point of a picket-fence headboard. Choose a wall color or wallpaper that contrasts with the pickets' crisp white and strong repetitive shapes. A cool, solid wall color recalls the serenity of shady, secluded gardens while a floral wallpaper sets a lively, animated ambience. Choose a repeating dominant color for your linens, then pair floral patterns with solids, stripes, and checks.

▶ Need a solution for a small room? Angle your
bed frame in a corner. Measure behind the bed
from wall to wall and purchase precut pickets to fit.
Nail pickets to two 2X4s for support and attach
with screws to the bed frame. For storage, include
a chest for a bedside table and a blanket trunk.

Table of favorite things

meld the practical with the decorative for this instant, inexpensive birdbath table. You'll enjoy the luxury of a handy surface for your books, magazines, reading glasses, or even a small lamp. And you'll have a safe place to display small objects and mementos. Pair your table with the most relaxing of all porch furniture—the classic rocking chair. As a finishing touch, sew an accent pillow from a garden-motif tea towel. Here, the towel's natural linen background and brick red accents complement the worn finish of the oak rocker.

1. Purchase a vintage or new birdbath. Terra-cotta, as shown here, or cast concrete birdbaths from nurseries or home centers are economical. For a hint of color, terra-cotta and cast concrete can be aged by rubbing on water-diluted latex paint.

◄ **2.** Fill the bowl with shiny pebbles, river rock, seed balls, tiny vine balls, seashells, marbles, or other small objects. Arrange seed packets, postcards, old photographs, gardening tools—whatever you like and enjoy carefully displaying.

► **3.** Purchase a precut, round ½-inch glass top from an import, crafts, or discount store. The 24-inch-diameter size works well for an average-size birdbath. For stability and safety, the bowl and base may be glued together with a household silicon adhesive.

chapter four

Art and accessories

Take your inspiration from the garden and the woodlands for projects beautiful in their simplicity. Whether you prefer shopping, crafting, or decorating with finds from the outdoors, decorate your home with natural motifs. A wooden or pottery bowl brimming with autumn leaves or fall vegetables is a stunning accessory that reflects the bounty of the season. In early spring, fill a tall vase, urn, or pitcher with branches ready to bloom. In winter, enjoy the stark beauty of bare branches. When you shop thrift stores or flea markets, look for botanical prints or for dilapidated books or scrapbooks with pages that can be separated and framed. For easy projects, buy pressed flowers or press your own. Decorate wooden plaques and boxes from crafts stores with pressed herbs. Combine a walk in the woods with a search for the twigs, leaves, and pinecones needed to craft your own innovative lamps and picture or mirror frames. If you enjoy the whimsical, age a small garden ornament for a lamp base. Aging techniques convert new ornaments into objects of beauty that are at home inside and out.

Art from pressed herbs

design art as personal as your home with dried herbs from the garden. Choose your favorite outdoor motif, such as a dragonfly, or arrange your own bouquet of herbs and blossoms. For canvases, start with unpainted wooden trays from the crafts store. Craft several trays to hang on your wall with plate hangers or display on stands. Purchase assorted pressed flowers at crafts stores. Or make your own with conventional or newer microwave flower presses—or by pressing blooms between the pages of telephone books.

◀ **1.** Sand and prime unpainted, crafts store wooden trays. Paint the entire tray with a base coat of interior latex paint. For an aged look, purchase a commercial crackle medium from a crafts or paint store. Carefully follow the directions on the bottle to apply.

◀ **2.** Follow directions on crackle medium for applying top coat. Load brush with paint and apply one coat in even strokes. For best results, do not reapply the top coat. As a decorative effect, detail the tray's trim in a third color. Allow to dry overnight.

▶ **3.** Arrange herbs on the tray until you like the design. If pieces overlap, glue the bottom pieces first. Squirt white crafts glue into a dish and apply to the herbs with a No. 2 round artist's brush. When the tray is dry, seal with water-based polyurethane.

Craft your garden style

1. See the watering can stencil pattern and instructions on page 165. Or select your own garden-style motif and copy to desired size. Tape the paper to the back side of the glass with the image showing through.

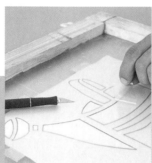

2. Apply clear contact paper to the front of the glass. Use a crafts knife to cut the image from contact paper. Remove paper from the back of the glass. Peel off sections of contact paper so the design shows through.

3. Follow the directions on glass etching cream purchased at a crafts store. Wear latex gloves. Apply the cream to warm glass with an artist's brush. Allow to etch according to directions. Rinse with warm soapy water. Remove contact paper.

base a pair of easy indoor-outdoor decorating projects on the beloved garden style accessories of watering cans and birdhouses. Use the projects together, as on this screened porch, or separately to decorate your favorite garden style space. The appeal of the outdoors is in the easy mix of motifs. To enhance the garden themes, incorporate watering cans, old tools, and collected birdhouses in several styles and materials. Paint and detail birdhouses in other color combinations—with or without rustic pebble roofs.

2. Allow birdhouse to completely dry. Dilute white or off-white latex paint with water or glaze and rub on with a clean cotton rag. If you are using outside, seal with two coats of polyurethane.

▶ **1.** Purchase an unfinished birdhouse. Sand and prime. Paint with latex paint. Apply crackle medium according to bottle directions. Brush on one coat of a contrasting paint.

▼ **3.** Pick up pebbles or flat rocks along creeks. Or buy similar stones at home or landscape centers. Starting at the bottom of the roofline, attach with clear silicon glue. Overlap for a shingled effect.

BIRD PAINTING   VOL II   CHRISTINE E JAC[...]

Collecting birdhouses

be kind to these helpful visitors to your garden with a snug house or a village of charming miniature cottages. Shop flea markets, fairs, and antiques shops for vintage birdhouses. Look for little houses that copy popular period architectural styles and local building materials—with details as realistic as columns, siding, chimneys, and tin

roofs. Or enjoy folk art birdhouses, crafted from all sorts of recycled materials and cast-offs. If you can't find just what you want in the old, look for new birdhouses in gardening catalogs, home centers, and plant nurseries. Feel free to enjoy the houses as art. Collect your favorite styles and colors for a bookshelf, mantel, or tabletop.

From the woodland garden

1. Antique a clean garden ornament. Make the glaze by diluting latex paint with water. Rub on with a clean cotton rag. Paint details, such as eyes, with undiluted paint. Purchase a base at a crafts store. Have the lamp wired at a lamp shop.

2. Attach the garden ornament to the wired lamp base with epoxy glue. For the small lamp feet, glue ½-inch wood plugs, used to fill screw holes, to the lamp base. Choose a lamp shade in a suitable decorative material, such as parchment.

Soothe a reading nook with lamps that recall shady garden paths and shy woodland creatures. This woodsy look fits with gardening trends to natural plantings and easy-maintenance native plants. The twig lamp, handsome in a bungalow living room, works well for porch reading, too. And the nut-gathering chipmunks would be fun in a child's room or garden-themed nursery.

1. Use wooden rounds with precut holes in center, threaded metal rod, and purchased lamp kit. Dry bundled twigs indoors for about a month. Rubber band them around the threaded rod. Wrap twine around branches and glue with white crafts glue.

2. Remove rubber bands from around the twigs. Cut twigs into segments for the lamp height and glue with white glue around the base. For small feet, glue ½-inch wood plugs to the base.

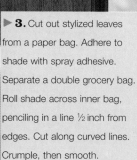

3. Cut out stylized leaves from a paper bag. Adhere to shade with spray adhesive. Separate a double grocery bag. Roll shade across inner bag, penciling in a line ½ inch from edges. Cut along curved lines. Crumple, then smooth.

4. Coat paper with spray adhesive and attach to shade. Use crafts glue to glue seam. Cut excess paper on edges to ½-inch beyond shade. Curl paper edges and glue to inside of shade. Brush on coat of amber shellac over entire shade.

No-sew floral treatments

keep your windows open to fresh air and garden views with treatments as light and natural as your decorating style. Banish anything heavy and ornate. If privacy or sun control aren't concerns, hang breezy unlined draperies, sheers, or lace panels. If the windows require coverage for privacy, install louvered shutters, roll-up bamboo or wooden blinds, or unfussy Roman shades. Narrow-slat blinds or bifold shutters pair well with fabric treatments or sheers. Branches and bamboo poles substitute nicely for standard drapery rods.

1. Shop linen outlets or sales for striped twin flat sheets. Choose a light color. Purchase a commercial sunburst-pattern rubber stamp and two ink pads in colors that blend with your scheme. Randomly stamp the sheets, alternating colors.

▼ **2.** Install a standard wooden drapery rod and bracket. Natural wood works well for the garden-style look. Loop the ends of the sheets over the rod to create a graceful swag. Bind and tie neatly with hemmed fabric, raffia, twine, or decorative grosgrain ribbon.

1. Raid your linen closet or shop flea markets, garden-style shops, or thrift stores for vintage tablecloths. The bright designs typically feature fruits or flowers or a combination. Or look for reproduction picnic cloths at linen shops or through catalogs.

2. Fold the cloth in half to make a triangle. Pin the valance to the window frame with decorative drapery tacks. If you need to cover multiple windows and don't have matching cloths, include checkered cloths in one of the colors of your floral pattern.

The art of garden finds

elevate the humble to art with well-edited arrangements of your finds. Framed pages from a

scrapbook of dried flowers unearthed in a secondhand store, proves the strength in numbers

of grid arrangements. So, too, do the more casual groupings of black-and-white garden

photographs on aged wire garden edging and vintage seed packets, chosen for their

shades of green, tacked above a desk with push pins. Stacked clay pots complete the theme.

Aging outdoor ornaments

1. Purchase a cast garden plaque with raised decorative detailing. Wipe with a damp rag to remove dust and allow to dry. Brush on a coat of off-white flat latex paint. Allow the painted plaque to dry thoroughly.

2. Mix one part latex glazing liquid to four parts grayish-green latex paint. Paint about one-third of the panel at a time. As you work, blot and dab with a clean cotton rag. If the glaze seems too thick or thin, adjust by adding more paint or more glaze.

3. Rub the glaze into crevices and dab off excess paint on the raised detailing to mimic the effects of aging. Add more glaze if needed. After the plaque dries, finish with three coats of clear, flat sealer. Allow drying time between coats.

aged garden ornaments evoke a sense of shady retreats, of sylvan pleasures lost among overgrown foliage. These wonderful old pieces, featured in garden antiques shows and shops around the country, are prized for their worn beauty. But if you can't locate the right ornament for your garden, patio, or porch, age your own affordable, easy-to-find plaques or statues, such as the popular cherub shown here, as well as assorted pots and planters. Directions include color choices and vary for your indoor-outdoor style.

1. Paint a cast concrete garden statue with off-white paint. Brush on, then rub in paint. If the concrete is porous, seal this base coat with clear sealer. Reapply the top coat if necessary for coverage.

2. Mix three to four parts caramel-colored paint to one part latex glazing liquid. Adjust with paint or glaze as needed. Rub on with a clean rag. Allow to dry. Dab on patches of diluted white base paint. Blend. Seal with a semigloss sealer.

Recall autumn glories

Every season contributes the beauty of nature and the garden to your home. Enjoy the mellow richness of fall year-round with projects inspired by autumn walks and crisp October days. These quick-to-craft frames contribute texture to your interiors and are interesting as decorative accessories. Or install glass and display a print, sepia-tone photograph, or pressed leaves or flowers. Add autumn leaves, scattered on a sideboard or a table, or fill a bowl with nuts, vine balls, pine cones, apples, or small fall vegetables.

◄ Scour salvage yards and secondhand shops for metal fence ornaments, such as these leaves, that can be attached with hot-glue adhesive to a frame. (Tiny clay pots or miniature garden tools can substitute.) Sand an old wood frame, then rub on diluted white paint.

► For the larger frame, paint twigs from the garden and join with twine and finishing nails. Pick up pinecones of various shapes and sizes and wrap with wire as a decorative garland. Twist around the frame. As a rustic accent for a small framed photograph, hot-glue mitered twigs as shown.

Frame a garden-style view

Incorporate old windows into your collecting and decorating mix. Interesting in their shapes and finishes, windows also work as screens that add depth to a table arrangement without blocking views and light. Hinge together pairs—or trios—of windows for free-standing potting-table screens. Place taller windows in a corner as a backdrop for potted plants. Choose windows of the same size and shape for stability. Or, for a three-panel screen, look for a taller or an arched window as the centerpiece for a pair of side windows. Vestiges of paint color and chipped layers contribute to the aged effect.

▶ **1.** Hunt salvage yards and antiques malls for multiples of old windows with muntin bars. Brush off loose paint with soft-bristled brushes. Clean with vinegar and water. Use a damp cotton swab to clean dirt-caked corners.

2. Purchase small brass hinges to connect windows. Use two hinges for each pair for stability. Measure and mark hinge locations with a tape measure and pencil. Drill pilot holes. Attach hinges with a screwdriver.

▶ **3.** Angle windows on a table top or floor. If you are concerned about scratching a wood surface, glue two or three small strips of felt to each window. If you have young children or pets, make sure the window screen is out of reach to prevent tipping over.

Creative collecting

Creativity makes garden-style collecting all the more fun. Look for multiples of like objects,
such as the metal flower arranging frogs (above), and group for dramatic impact. Search for
a range of finishes and textures for an evocative mood. Gently aged silver-plate trays and
candelabras, combined with lush plants, imbue your setting with the spirit of an overgrown
tropical garden. Worn metal folding chairs contribute patina and an insouciant attitude.

Paint a pretty tole tray

decorated with floral motifs, tole trays add a sense of never-ending garden parties to any room. Collectors shop favorite flea markets and antiques stores for the prized accessory to group on walls and tabletops. If you like the look, paint a tray or two in your own color palette. As the flowers and bouquets are stylized, even a beginner can create beautiful trays worthy of display. You'll also be able to use whites and lighter pastel colors popular with current decorating trends. The secret? Shop junk stores for good buys in old metal trays.

◀ **1.** Lightly sand, clean, and prime old metal trays with latex primer recommended for metal. Allow to dry. Paint with a latex base coat. To simulate aging, rub a candle over the dry tray. Concentrate on the corners and the edges of the tray.

▶ **2.** Paint a top coat with latex paint. Allow to dry. Place a drop cloth or newspapers under the tray to neatly catch sanded dust. Choose colors in pleasing combinations, such as shades of lilac, pale green, and sunny yellow that emulate the garden.

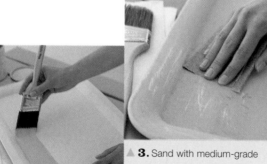

▲ **3.** Sand with medium-grade sandpaper. This causes the top coat to sand off wherever the wax was applied, exposing the base coat. Sand with a smooth, light motion so that the base layer, but not the metal, is exposed under the top coat.

▶ **4.** Purchase artist's acrylic paint in your color choices and small artist's brushes. Choose a simple motif and practice first on scrap paper. Paint flowers, leaves, and stems. Fill in and add detail with darker shades of paint. Accent with black paint.

Plants, pots, planters

Inside and out, plants and their containers are key elements of garden style. You'll find endless choices from the stark beauty of unglazed terra-cotta pots to imported glazed cachepots to metal urns and wooden planters. Shopping venues are equally varied for new and vintage containers. If the charm of workaday clay pots appeals to you, consider the more decorative ones with applied or cast designs that are often found at garden centers and nurseries. Garden style devotees naturally gravitate to the decorative glazed flowerpots mass produced from the 1920s through the 1950s. Best-known makers include McCoy Pottery, which stamped pots with its well-recognized name. Such flowerpots, some with integral saucers, were manufactured in stylized motifs and glazes in pastels and dark greens. Keep re-purposing in mind when you search for ideas for containers. Vintage and new watering cans are naturals for plants and seasonal flowers. So are galvanized tubs, buckets, and enamelware pitchers. Remember large baskets, wooden boxes, fruit crates, and small wagons and wheelbarrows when you display your plants in style.

▶ **1.** Put on protective eyewear. Break plates or fragments by covering with a cloth and hitting with a hammer. Use a tile nipper to cut pieces to size. Apply adhesive glue to the back of each piece; press against the pot. Allow pot to dry overnight.

Make your own mosaics

Cry no more over broken pottery or porcelain. Instead, recycle bits and pieces of a beloved plate, cup, or vase into a stylish mosaic pot. If you can't wait until you save enough shards, purchase cracked or chipped pieces at garage sales and secondhand shops, and make your own fragments (see directions below). Limit yourself to a two-color scheme, such as easy-to-find blue and white, or design your favorite color and pattern combinations. For a shower or luncheon table, craft a small pot for each place setting. Or fill with a blooming plant or wrapped candies for a creative hostess gift.

◀ 2. Apply premixed grout from a hardware store or home center to the entire surface of a clean, dry pot. Make sure you completely fill between the shards of pottery for a unified look. If you prefer, leave the rim exposed for decorative contrast.

◀ 3. Use a tile float to smooth and even out the grout. Allow the pot to dry for several hours. A hazy film of dried grout will appear on tile. Carefully wipe away the film with a damp sponge. Rinse out sponge as needed.

▶ 4. Allow the pot to dry for a week. When you are sure the grout is completely dry, seal with a grout sealer. These pots are ideal for silverware and napkins for parties, or as desk or potting shed accessories for pencils and pens or tools respectively.

finding
&
displaying

Potting shed pleasures

relish the solitude of your potting shed—or potting corner—with plenty of storage to orga-

nize the essentials. Keeping your materials in order makes work more fun. If space allows, add

a cabinet for concealed storage. Use the walls to hang the practical and the decorative.

1. Transplant a well-rooted rosemary plant into sterilized potting soil. Clip lower ancillary growth, leaving lower two-thirds bare. Clip off the terminal shoot.

2. Stake, tie, and place in a sunny, well-protected spot. Loosen the ties as the stem grows. Turn every week so the top grows in a round, even shape. Water when dry. Grow several topiaries for centerpieces and as hostess gifts.

Plant decorative topiaries

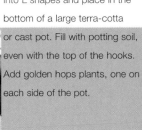

1. Bend two coat hangers into L shapes and place in the bottom of a large terra-cotta or cast pot. Fill with potting soil, even with the top of the hooks. Add golden hops plants, one on each side of the pot.

2. Position one tomato cage over the other. Hold top cage and make a quarter turn. Place cages firmly in the soil, attaching to coat hanger hooks. With pliers, squeeze hooks shut over cage frame. Push frame into the soil.

3. Reach through the cage to plant blue morning glory or other annual or perennial vines. Secure a topiary form to the top of the cages or tie cage spikes with wire or twine. Pinch back and wind plants so the bottom fills in. Water daily in summer.

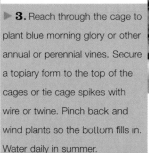

i ndoors on sunny windowsills or outdoors in the garden, topiaries infuse your favorite setting with well-mannered charm. Plant multiples of small- and medium-size topiaries to group as impromptu centerpieces or to relieve the boredom of long winters. Useful herb topiaries recall the hospitable tables and casually elegant decorating of France and Italy. Larger outdoor topiaries give the often-needed focal point to a garden. To block a view or create a lush backdrop, plant large, full topiaries and group for impact.

Clay pots old and new

the most utilitarian and widely produced of all garden elements, terra-
cotta pots trace their history to the
most ancient civilizations. If you
enjoy collecting, look for the English
Victorian-era pots found in shops that
sell vintage garden ornaments and
tools. Or search junk shops, flea markets, tag sales, and your own garage or

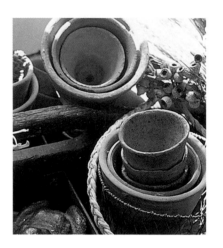

basement for pots and saucers. Prized today are those that were painted and repainted and now exhibit fashionable layers of roughly peeling paint. Brush off flaking paint and wash with soap and water. New clay pots contribute their own charms. Shop for plain ones to stack, or for designs with raised or applied decorative details.

Create a miniature garden

1. In a large bucket of water, soak moss, one sheet at a time, for about a minute. Carefully remove; wring until damp-dry. Starting at the back section, press moss into place on the wire basket. (See page 165 for a mail-order basket source.)

2. Continue until entire basket is lined with moss. Spray adhesive to attach pieces of moss to each other at the two corners. Don't skip this step as it's important for the sheets of moss to adhere properly to the wire basket for a neat look.

3. Arrange an assortment of herbs in 2- to 3-inch plastic growers pots. Don't remove from pots. Place trailing herbs in front and allow to spill over the basket. Cover pots with remaining moss and attach a ribbon to the top of the basket.

e asy to work with and inexpensive, moss provides a natural container or base for plants. Use versatile moss from a nursery or flower shop to line wire baskets, window boxes, and planters. Moss retains moisture and creates an attractive setting for green and seasonal blooming plants. Or use moss as the landscape for tabletop terrariums or tiny rock gardens. Cover exposed potting soil in houseplants with a thin layer of decorative moss. Place around the plant and wedge neatly into your pot or container. An occasional spritz of water helps the moss to stay fresh and green.

1. Convert a decorative cake stand with domed cover into a terrarium garden. (Look for reproduction stands at discount stores or shop thrift stores and tag sales.) Cover the base with a layer of natural moss collected from a creek bed.

2. Add rocks and pebbles in several sizes and shapes. Gather on nature walks and wash or purchase pebbles at nurseries or craft stores. You may want to add other natural elements such as twigs, pinecones, pieces of bark, or small, delicate seashells.

3. Spritz with water, making sure the entire area is well-moistened. Cover and enjoy a touch of green any time of year. To keep the dome looking fresh and green, spritz every few weeks, or when you notice the moss is starting to look a little dry.

Create a sunroom mood

relax your dining room with the help of re-purposed outdoor pieces. Start with a cheerful yellow background. Here, a metal grate, on stand, is transformed into a durable table for topiaries, while a wire plant stand neatly contains sun-loving houseplants on a tray and

Plant pots of spring green

Whatever the calendar or the temperature, spring seems only two or three weeks away when you plant pots of fast-growing grass seed. Plant a mix of pots from miniatures to rectangular planters. Embellish with transplanted tulips or paperwhites during late fall or winter. Include annuals, lilies, or small perennials for springtime and summer. The pots are so easy and inexpensive you'll want to plant them as winter pick-me-ups for friends or for party centerpieces and one-of-a-kind favors. Tie with raffia for a finishing touch.

◄ 1. Gather a collection of terra-cotta pots and saucers in varying or matching sizes. Add pebbles to the bottom of each pot and fill with a good-quality potting soil mixed with peat. (Small pots can be filled with soil only.)

◄ 2. Sprinkle grass seeds on top of the soil. Any type of annual grass seed will work. Annual rye grows faster than other varieties. Place the pots in a bright location, such as a sill, and water when the soil begins to dry out.

► 3. Trim with scissors as needed. Start pots every two to three weeks for a winter of constant greenery. For centerpieces, insert tulips or other blooms using plastic water picks that hold a single bloom.

Emulate weathered effects

1. Choose a plastic planter with detailing. Brush on a gray-tinted exterior latex paint. Allow to dry at least four hours; reapply. Allow the second coat to dry an additional four hours. A good base is key to a handsome finish.

2. Mix three parts medium-gray exterior latex paint to one part black. Stir together until blended but with streaks remaining. With quick motions, apply a thin coat. Allow some of the base to show, especially around the grooves. Allow to dry.

3. Dip brush into white exterior latex paint. Very lightly brush on streaks for a chalky finish. Apply paint sparingly during this step. Allow to dry for three or four hours and seal with a coat of polyurethane.

1. Prime your bucket, planter, watering can, or other container with a primer formulated for metal. Allow to dry. Brush on a coat of gold acrylic paint from a crafts store. Allow to dry.

2. Brush on a coat of umber acrylic paint from the crafts store. Allow to dry. This layer should not be solid; some gold should show through. If the first stroke appears too opaque, dilute paint with clear glaze. Brush on and allow to dry.

3. With a dry brush, brush on aqua latex paint. If it appears too opaque, dilute with glaze. Some of the gold and umber should show through. Allow to dry. Seal with two or three coats of water-based polyurethane.

With paint and practice, you can turn basic, inexpensive metal and plastic into high-style garden containers. If you like verdigris, the wonderfully aged effect of copper exposed to the elements, try the decorative imitation, above. Or if you prefer the classic look of English lead urns, paint the lightweight, weather-resistant version, opposite, based on economical plastic pots.

Pots decorative and aged

Stacked or planted, glazed or painted, flowerpots exemplify the idea of bringing the outdoors inside. For some collectors, the fun comes from assembling flowerpots from one manufacturer, such as the well-known glazed McCoy pottery featured on this page. Other collectors enjoy amassing pots of specific motifs, shapes, or colors. For those who relish the rustic charm of the outdoors, well-worn terra-cotta pots with layers of flaking paint are their rewards for searching tag sales and secondhand stores.

◀ In the late 1920s, McCoy Pottery started firing pots with blended glazes and stylized plant motifs. Inexpensive and colorful, the marked pots were sold by flower shops through the 1950s. Pots with and without saucers are still affordable and easy to find in antiques shops and at shows, but prices are rising.

▶ Weathered, chipping pots are the good buys of garden-style collecting. If you don't mind dust and cobwebs, rescue them from the bargain basements of antiques stores, junk shops, and antiques malls. Clean up your finds and plant with long-blooming annuals, such as pansies, petunias, or marigolds.

Tools of toil and soil

hand trowels, forks, shears, and garden-hose nozzles of all sorts are bargains of garden-style decorating. Add rakes, spades, hoes, and children's tools, and your collection widens. Metal tools from the 1930s through the 1950s were sometimes painted in bright colors. Left in the elements, old tools have the worn and rusted finishes that

bespeak their own hardworking pasts. Some vintage hand tools can still be found for less than $10 each; old hose nozzles in assorted sizes are buys when you find them for $5 or so. Besides shops, shows, and flea markets, collectors make tools a priority when they shop tag, garage, and rummage sales. And you can garden with them too.

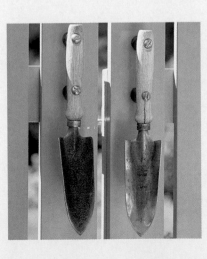

1. Start with a clean, dry, terra-cotta pot. Mark pencil points on the rim and bottom for spacing. Hand-paint stripes with white enamel, using the width of the brush for spacing. Choose the stripe and brush according to the size of the clay pot.

2. Paint the rim of the pot with white enamel. Allow the paint to dry thoroughly and brush on an acrylic fixative. For an interesting combination, paint the stripe motifs on pots of varying sizes. Smaller ones are ideal for tabletop decorating and gifts.

Painted pots as garden art

1. Wear rubber gloves. Pour one part water into a mixing container. Shake in two parts Portland cement. Add one part concrete bonding adhesive. Mix to the consistency of heavy whipping cream. Brush onto the ribbed side of the leaf.

▼ **2.** Press the leaf to the dry pot with your fingers, then with a damp sponge. Wipe away mix that seeps out. Leave on for one to two minutes. Carefully peel away the leaf. Reuse the leaf or decorate your pots with leaves of different sizes and shapes.

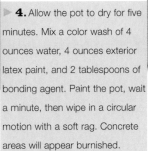

◀ **3.** Hold the leaf in place on the rim of the pot. Brush around the leaf with the mixture. Try silhouetting around the rim. If you aren't happy with the look, wipe off and try again or touch up problem spots with a small artist's brush.

▶ **4.** Allow the pot to dry for five minutes. Mix a color wash of 4 ounces water, 4 ounces exterior latex paint, and 2 tablespoons of bonding agent. Paint the pot, wait a minute, then wipe in a circular motion with a soft rag. Concrete areas will appear burnished.

dress up your basic terra-cotta pots with paint and easy techniques. Choose the look and colors to fit your own garden-decorating scheme. Sporty stripes recall awnings and garden parties while reverse-stenciled leaves evoke the mood of cool, shady retreats. For natural aging, paint the pots, then leave outside to weather through the summer. Or, if you want to preserve a pristine, freshly painted finish, seal with a coat or two of a clear acrylic. For variety, mix with pots painted in solid colors and pots left unadorned.

Plant a lush window box

give your home or potting shed instant detailing with an old-fashioned window box. Add

applied decorative trim to dress up a plain box. Or put your own one together from recycled

wood. (Be sure to include drainage holes and a liner for easy transplanting.) For the romance

of a cottage garden, include flowing vines, such as ivy, with two or three varieties of

seasonal blooming flowers. Replenish as needed through the seasons. Water often and enjoy.

1. Prime a bucket with metal primer. Allow to dry. Base paint with your darkest color. Mask off and paint stripes with a lighter, coordinating color, such as a paler tint of the same cool green. Allow to dry completely.

▼ **2.** Cut images from note cards or heavy gift wrap. Brush the backs with decoupage medium; press in place. Rub images to remove bubbles. Coat surface with decoupage medium. Allow to dry. Apply as many as 10 coats, drying between each.

Start with tin containers

W hen you need a decorative houseplant container for your living or dining room or as a gift for a friend, craft your own stylish metal one. Painted metal containers, such as tole cachepots, have long been popular decorating accessories in traditional-style rooms. With these natural motifs based on flowers and fall leaves, the look is more relaxed and playful. For entertaining, fill with ice to chill wine, beer, or soft drink bottles.

1. Punch holes in the bucket rim with an awl and hammer. Wrap copper wire around stones. With needle-nose pliers, wrap the long tail of wire around the uncut wire end. Insert wire end through holes in the bucket and attach to assorted stone beads.

2. Gather fall leaves or purchase colorful paper leaves. Brush rubber cement on the backs of leaves and apply to the container. Arrange casually over the surface of the container. Rub with a soft rag to secure the leaves in place.

Relaxed entertaining

Few pleasures in life exceed dining or relaxing on a shady porch or under a bright, starry sky. From brunches and birthday parties to romantic candlelight dinners, a fresh-air setting makes any occasion all the more memorable. As outdoor entertaining lends itself to a casual mood, planning, preparation, and cleanup are easy. With the garden and outdoors as a backdrop, a few well-chosen touches, such as luminarias or lanterns, or a candle chandelier hung from a tree, set a getaway mood. Projects are fun with a garden-style theme. Incorporate daisy-painted straw hats and stamped daisies to dress up folding chairs and a tablecloth. Take such themes inside for lighthearted entertaining when the weather isn't cooperating. When time is tight, just bring in a metal garden table or two, top with bright and festive tablecloths, and add folding garden chairs with floral or print pillows. With blooming plants in painted clay pots, you'll feel as though you are dining in the garden, whatever the season or the temperature. Garden-style entertaining—like garden-style decorating—is most of all a state of mind.

Roses by candlelight

roses and candlelight whisper romance. Combine them for an idyllic setting as perfect for a special occasion outdoor party as they are for an intimate dinner for two. Choose a secluded setting, shaded by a tree with sturdy limbs low enough to gracefully suspend a candle chandelier. Bring out a table and comfortable chairs. Or make your serving piece by topping a stable base with a door from a salvage yard. Decorate with roses, ivy, fruit, and architectural fragments. For gatherings, dress a candelabra with pots of roses.

◄ **1.** Shop for a candle chandelier at shops that sell garden ornaments. Measure the length of chain you need and have it cut to fit at a hardware store or home center. Attach securely to the chandelier and loop it over a sturdy limb.

◄ **2.** For a candelabra, cut roses and place in florist picks. Fill small terra-cotta pots with florist foam. Push in picks and cover with moss. Add pots of English ivy to twine through the candelabra. For sources of antique ornaments, see page 165.

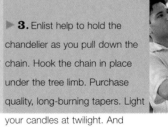

► **3.** Enlist help to hold the chandelier as you pull down the chain. Hook the chain in place under the tree limb. Purchase quality, long-burning tapers. Light your candles at twilight. And savor a long summer evening under a romantic starry sky.

Easy, elegant luncheon table

Whose apple pie recipe won a blue ribbon in the 1952 State Fair?

Start with white and add your favorite garden or florist flower for inviting tabletops. For a large gathering, cover tables with white sheets and dress with an overlay of sheer tulle from the fabric store. Mix and match white dinnerware and clear or cut glasses. A variety of china patterns livens up the scene. Collect white pitchers, tureens, and vases and fill with arrangements of a single flower. For cards at the place settings, fold two layers of medium-weight paper in your colors and stitch with gold cord. Hand-write or stamp.

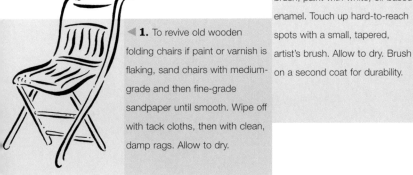

◀ 1. To revive old wooden folding chairs if paint or varnish is flaking, sand chairs with medium-grade and then fine-grade sandpaper until smooth. Wipe off with tack cloths, then with clean, damp rags. Allow to dry.

▶ 2. Prime the wood. Using a brush, paint with white, oil-based enamel. Touch up hard-to-reach spots with a small, tapered, artist's brush. Allow to dry. Brush on a second coat for durability.

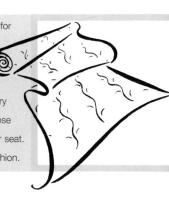

▶ 3. Cut a plywood base for the cushion. Cover with foam. Cut vinyl to fit; staple to underside of the base. Attach with upholstery tacks and/or general purpose household glue to the chair seat. Or tie on a small fabric cushion.

High tea in the garden

1. Look for an architectural salvage etagérè. (A three-tier metal plate rack can substitute.) Fill a decorative pot with potting soil mixed with vermiculite or peat. Transplant an 8-inch pot of ivy. Choose a full plant with tendrils 30 to 36 inches long.

2. Place the pot on the bottom shelf and arrange tendrils evenly around the legs of the etagérè. Begin twining the tendrils up one leg of the etagérè or plate rack. Repeat, with another tendril up the same leg, rotating the ivy in the opposite twining direction.

3. Continue until all the legs are twined to the decorative top. Twine the shorter tendrils from the top for fullness. Leave several smaller tendrils trailing outside the sides of the pot for a lush, finished topiary. Place a saucer underneath for watering.

invite guests for a treat—tea in your garden. Move a table and chairs from your porch to a scenic spot and add a colorful cloth and tea set. To set the tone of an English garden in summer, decorate with a stylish architectural salvage topiary you make yourself. Fill white pitchers with flowers from your garden or a mix of blooms from a farmer's market. The idea translates well into other settings. For a deck, balcony, or patio, plant a variety of containers with annuals and vines a month in advance for a lush garden effect.

Gifts from the outdoors

▶ Decorate for a party or an outdoor wedding with hanging baskets made from large ivy or other leaves. Roll into a cone shape and staple together at the top. Add a handle from a blooming vine, such as jasmine. Fill with blooms in water-filled florists vials. For an outdoor wedding, add birdseed for guests to scatter.

Shop in your garden when you need a quick hostess gift or favors for your own party. Look for leaves, vines, blooms, and buds to quickly craft into miniature arrangements. Visit a flower shop or nursery to fill in with extra flowers, bulbs, and pebbles, and you'll have all the materials you need to make charming gifts. Experiment with leaves as fairylike hanging vases or decorative coverings for boxes of all shapes and sizes. Collect tiny clear and colored bottles, tie with vines or raffia, and fill with sprigs of buds, wildflowers, and herbs.

For a gift or centerpiece, cover a kraft-paper box with galax or ivy leaves. Coat the backs of the just-cut leaves with spray adhesive and overlap to completely cover the paper. Fill the box with a bed of moss for bulbs and blooms, such as this delicate freesia. Or add pebbles and buds in florist picks.

Wine tasting at sunset

entertain easily and stylishly with a wine tasting at twilight. As the light fades on a long afternoon, light the candles on this distinctive topiary and unwind to soft music. Cover your patio table with a printed tablecloth and decorate with parsley from the garden as an alternative to cut flowers. Incorporate your refreshments into the tablescape by filling a compote with fruits of the season. Mix an array of wineglasses and let your party begin. If weather is inclement, move the party to your dining room for a taste of summer.

◀ 1. Transplant an 8-inch ivy plant with long tendrils to a terracotta pot with a drainage hole. Add high-quality potting soil to fill in. Insert a candelabra topiary form into the center of the plant. (See page 165 for mail-order topiary-form sources.)

◀ 2. Locate the longest ivy tendril and twine around the stem of the topiary form. Continue up the longest candelabra arm. Repeat with a second tendril, twining in the opposite direction. Continue until the topiary form is completely covered with ivy.

▶ 3. Leave the short tendrils around the base of the topiary to frame the pot. Place round candles in the designated candle slots. Add moss around the base of the topiary to cover the potting soil. Water the topiary thoroughly to keep it fresh.

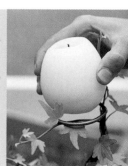

Alfresco dining at dusk

Set a memorable scene for your next fresh-air gathering. The secret? Decorate your porch, terrace, or garden hideaway—at least for the evening—with all the comforts of the indoors. Define your space with a sisal rug. Cover a table with a colorful cotton print, soften a chair with a floral cushion or stylized quilt. Light a corner of the garden with candles. If you don't have a chandelier, substitute candle stakes or lamp-oil torches from import stores.

Tin can party luminarias

decorate your deck for your next party or cookout with an array of quick ideas. For a backdrop for a serving table, hang or lean salvaged shutters against the wall of your house. Enliven with a planted hanging basket. (Mix blooming annuals, green plants, and hanging vines for a festive effect.) If you have time, plant a large metal watering can with trailing, flowering vines. Light the setting with decoratively punched luminarias crafted from cans and terra-cotta saucers. Add votive candles and welcome family and friends.

◄ **1.** Remove labels, tops, and bottoms of 26-ounce cans. Use an old-fashioned beer can opener to make triangular holes around the perimeter of the top and bottom of each can. Wear work gloves; beware of sharp edges.

2. With a hammer and sharp nail, carefully punch additional holes in a pattern on the surface of each can. Aim for simple, stylized patterns. Work with a spare can or two for practice.

◄ **3.** Place each can in a terra-cotta saucer with a votive candle inside. For taller bases, glue a pair of saucers bottom to bottom. Vary the tall and short bases on your deck, patio, and tabletop for lively decorative interest.

Re-purposed containers

fill the containers you find at your fingertips. You'll notice fresh flowers from your garden—or the neighborhood market—will become an essential part of your everyday life. If you don't have the right size vase for what you need for wild violets or early spring irises, commandeer what you do have. Different sizes and shapes of

jars, bottles, buckets, and cans are charming containers. Use cans or jars alone or arrange them together in flat baskets. Remember your little-used coffee or teapots or water pitchers from durable metals to fine china. For small-scale arrangements, fill a teapot from a child's tea set with wildflowers or delicate miniature roses.

Lunching in the garden

◀ Create a garden setting any time of year with Chippendale-style painted furniture made more comfortable with small, decorative pillows. Incorporate garden statuary into your centerpiece and include topiaries and topiary forms. Overlay crisp white on a colored cloth. And arrange glamourous white roses.

▶ Design an indoor tablescape with the easy starting point of Mediterranean blue, the shade associated with sun-drenched Provence and Tuscany. Paint wooden chairs, tie on blue-striped cushions, and shade with a garden umbrella. Take a break from prints with a pleated cloth trimmed in the stripes.

Picturesque gardens of England, France, and Italy inspire table settings appropriate for memorable occasions. Indoor versions welcome friends throughout the year and are especially inviting as respites from dreary winter days. Order flowers or force bulbs in advance to fill your dining room with scents and sights of spring. Add topiaries and ivy to complete the setting.

1. Purchase plain, wide-brimmed straw hats at a discount store. With an artist's brush, hand paint petals around the brim. If you are unsure about spacing, mark first so the petals are evenly spaced. Taper ends.

2. Attach green organza or other sheer ribbon to the hat. Cut at least 60 inches, depending on the width of the chair, so you can tie a generous bow. Secure tightly enough so that the hat doesn't slip.

Daisy of an outdoor party

1. Cut a square of gauze to comfortably fit your table. Unravel about ½-inch on each edge and run a line of fray-stopping product to prevent further unraveling. Carefully draw and cut out a 3-inch-diameter daisy from standard rubber foam.

2. Lay the fabric over paper. Coat one side of the stamp with fabric paint. Carefully press the stamp down and lift up. Fill in with a small brush. Repeat for each flower. Space evenly over the table overskirt for a happily random, cheerful look.

3. Allow the daisies to dry completely. Paint the center of each daisy with a yellow fabric paint. If you prefer, stamp yellow daisies and fill in with white centers. Or vary the sizes of the stamps with some larger, some smaller daisy motifs.

today's retro look at the 1960s inspires this garden party, based on the decade's favorite blossom. Like the '60s fashion in clothes, this party setting is based on having fun—and not taking anything too seriously. To re-create the setting, base your scheme on yellow, bright green, white—and lots of daisies. Paint inexpensive, wide-brimmed straw hats as decorations that double as party favors. Paint stripes on a terra-cotta pot, and dress your table with a gauze cloth dotted with stamped and hand-painted summer daisies.

Sources and credits

Pages 12-13: Project design: Sonja Carmon and Wade Scherrer; styling: Wade Scherrer, Des Moines, Iowa: fabric: Seabrook, Memphis, Tennessee (800/238-9152); iron table and chairs: My Sister Shabby's Place on Fifth, Des Moines, Iowa, 515/255-8022; photography: King Au/Studio Au, Des Moines, Iowa.

Pages 14-15: Project design and styling: Wade Scherrer; photography: King Au/Studio Au.

Page 17: Styling: Wade Scherrer; location: Jennifer Stoffel, My Sister Shabby's Place on Fifth; Photography: King Au/Studio Au.

Pages 18 and 19: Produced and photographed: Gridley and Graves, Easton, Pennsylvania. Steel lawn chair sources: pictured vintage chairs: Synthia's Antiques & Embellishments, Ventura, California, 805/641-2621; reproduction chairs: Lloyd/Flanders Industries, Inc., 800/526-9894; Crate & Barrel (catalog or store location): 888/249-4155; Target (store location): 800/800-8800.

Pages 20-21: Project design: Patricia Mohr Kramer, Ames, Iowa; salvage supplier: Roger Dahlstrom; photography: Pete Krumhardt, Des Moines, Iowa; Greg Scheideman, Des Moines, Iowa.

Pages 22-25: Project design, decorative painting, and location: Amy Queen, Missouri City, Texas; regional editor: Joetta Moulden, Houston, Texas; photography: Fran Brennan, Houston, Texas.

Pages 26-27: Project design and location: Anthony Kavanagh Antiques, Three Oaks, Michigan, 616/469-6569; regional editor: Sally Mauer, Northbrook, Illinois; photography: Bob Mauer, Evanston.

Page 28: Photography: Jamie Hadley, San Francisco, California.

Page 29: Photography: King Au/Studio Au.

Page 30: Photography: Barbara Martin, St Louis, Missouri.

Page 31: Project design: Brett McFarland, Des Moines, Iowa; photography: King Au/Studio Au.

Pages 34-35: Project design: Patricia Mohr Kramer; styling: Wade Scherrer; photography: King Au/Studio Au.

38-39: Stencil project: Patricia Mohr Kramer; Slipcovers and table runner projects: Sonja Carmon; Styling: Jennifer Stoffel, My Sister Shabby's Place on Fifth, West Des Moines Iowa and Wade Scherrer; location: My Sister Shabby's; photography: King Au/Studio Au.

Page 40: Decorating: Regional editor: Estelle Bond Guralnick, Boston, Massachusetts; Photography: Eric Roth, Topfield, Massachusetts.

Page 42: Regional editor: Nancy Ingram, Tulsa, Oklahoma; photography: Jenifer Jordan, Waxahachie, Texas.

Page 44: Handpainted wall project: Jennifer Stoffel; painted chest project: Elaine Miller, Des Moines, Iowa; styling: Wade Scherrer; location: My Sister Shabby's; photography: King Au/Studio Au.

Page 45: Regional editor: Andrea Caughey, San Diego, California; photographer: Ed Gohlich, Coronado.

Pages 46-47: photography: Jenifer Jordan.

Pages 48-49: Regional editor: Nancy Ingram; photography: Jenifer Jordan.

Pages 50-51: Project design and location: Pam Barrett, Austin, Texas; regional editor: Mary Baskin, Waco, Texas; photographer: Jenifer Jordan.

Page 52: Photography: Jamie Hadley.

Pages 54-55: regional editor: Mary Baskin; photographer: Jenifer Jordan.

Pages 58-59: Project design: Patricia Mohr Kramer; styling: Wade Scherrer; photography: King Au/Studio Au.

Pages 60-61: Regional editor: Mary Baskin; photography: Jenifer Jordan.

Pages 62-63: Regional editor: Mary Baskin; photography: Jenifer Jordan.

Page 64: Photography: Bill Holt, Larkspur, California.

Page 65: Regional contributor: Trish Maharam, Seattle, Washington; photography: Michael Jensen, Seattle.

Pages 66-67: Project design and location: Jennifer Stoffel; styling: Wade Scherrer; photography: King Au/Studio Au.

Pages 70-71: Project design: Patricia Mohr Kramer; photography: King Au/Studio Au.

Page 72: Regional contributor: Suzy Farbman, Detroit, Michigan; photography: Beth Singer, Detroit, Michigan.

Page 73: Photography: Jon Jensen, Portland, Oregon.

Page 74: Photography: Richard Felber, South Kent, Connecticut.

Page 75: Regional editor: Nancy Ingram; photography: Jenifer Jordan; photography: King Au/Studio Au.

Pages 76-77: Project design: Jennifer Stoffel; styling: Wade Scherrer; photography: King Au/Studio Au.

Pages 78-79: Source for distressed furniture and fragments: Hikchik, Walnut Street, West Des Moines, Iowa; 515/255-0588.

Page 80: Produced by Matthew Mead; photography: Jeff McNamara, Easton, Connecticut.

Page 81: Regional editor: Ann Bertelsen; photography: Jon Jensen.

Pages 82-83: Project design: Sonja Carmon; photography: Studio Au.

Page 84: Produced by Catherine Kramer; photography: Studio Au;

▶ Full size pattern for stenciled projects on pages 38-39.

Page 85 Photography: King Au/Studio Au and Jenifer Jordan.

Page 86: Photography: Jenifer Jordan.

Page 87: Project design: Rebecca Jerdee; photography: Studio Au.

Pages 88-89: Project design and styling: Wade Scherrer; photography: King Au/Studio Au.

Pages 92-93: Project design: Patricia Mohr Kramer; styling: Jennifer Stoffel and Wade Scherrer; photography: King Au/Studio Au.

Pages 94-95: Project design and styling: Wade Scherrer; photography: King Au/Studio Au.

Pages 98-99: Project design and styling: Wade Scherrer; photography: King Au/Studio Au.

Pages 100-101: Project design: Michele Michael; Photography: King Au/Studio Au.

Pages 102 and 103 (upper left): Produced by James Cramer and Dean Johnson; photography: William Stites, Marathon, Florida.

Pages 106-107: Produced by James Cramer and Dean Johnson; photography: Gary Graves.

Pages 108-109: Project design and location: Donna Wendt, Ivy Vine Topiaries & Garden Rooms Ltd., Saratoga Springs, New York, 518/587-9642. Styling: Heather Lobdell, Chevy Chase, Maryland; photography: Gordon Beall, Chevy Chase, Maryland.

Pages 110-111: Project design and location: Jacqui Stoneman, Utopia Antiques, Dallas, Texas 214/443-9999; regional editor: Mary Baskin; photography: Jenifer Jordan.

Pages 112-113: Project design: Patricia Mohr Kramer; photography: King Au/Studio Au.

Pages 116-117 Step-by-step photography: King Au/Studio Au.

Page 121: Regional editor: Trish Maharam; photography: Michael Jensen.

Page 124: Project design and location: Donna Wendt; styling: Heather Lobdell; photography: Gordon Beall. Mail-order topiary supplies: Ivy Vine Topiaries, 518/587-9642.

Page 125: Project design and styling: Wade Scherrer; photography: Studio Au.

Pages 126-127: Project design and location: Donna Wendt; styling: Heather Lobdell; photography: Gordon Beall.

Pages 128-129: Produced by Bonnie Maharam; photography: Bill Holt.

Page 130: Project design: Donna Wendt; photography: Gordon Beall.

Page 131: Project design: Patricia Mohr Kramer; styling: Jennifer Stoffel and Wade Scherrer; photography Studio Au.

Page 132: Photography: KingAu/StudioAu.

Page 136: Styling: Wade Scherrer; photography: King Au/Studio Au.

Page 137: Project design: George Little and David Lewis; Regional contributor: Loralee Wenger; photography: Michael Jensen.

Page 138: Produced by Donna Pizzi; photography: Philip Clayton-Thompson, Portland, Oregon.

Pages 140-141: Photography: Hopkins Associates, Des Moines.

Pages 144-145: Project and floral design: Chris Brown, Dallas, Texas; location and sources: Liberty & Sons Antiques Market, Dallas, Texas, 214/748-3329; regional editor: Mary Baskin; photography: Jenifer Jordan.

Pages 148-149: Project design and location: Donna Wendt; styling: Heather Lobdell; photography: Gordon Beall.

Pages 150-151: Produced by Michaele Thunen; photography: Mark Lund.

152-153: Project design and location: Donna Wendt; styling: Heather Lobdell; photography: Gordon Beall.

Page 154: Regional contributor: Trish Maharam; photography: Mike Jensen.

Page 155: Regional editor: Mary Anne Thomson; photography: Barbara Martin; styling: Brian Carter; photography: Emily Minton.

Pages 156-157: Project design and styling: Wade Scherrer; photography: King Au/Studio Au.

Page 160: Regional editor: Estelle Guralnik; photography: Eric Roth.

Page 161: Regional editor: Bonnie Maharam; phtography: Bill Holt.

Pages 162-163: Project design, styling and location: Brian Carter, Atlanta, Georgia; photography: Emily Minton, Atlanta, Georgia.

Special thanks:

Anthony Kavanagh Antiques: 101 Generation Drive;Three Oaks, Michigan 49128; 616/469-6569

Hikchik: 417 Maple St.; West Des Moines, Iowa; 515/255-0588

Ivy Vine Topiaries & Garden Rooms Ltd.: Saratoga Springs, New York; 518/587-9642

Liberty & Sons Antiques Market: 1506 Market Center Blvd.; Dallas, Texas 75207; 214/748-3329; fax: 214/748-4447

My Sister Shabby's Place on Fifth: 304 S. Fifth St.; West Des Moines, Iowa 50265; 515/255-8022 or 888/SHABBY-4

Utopia Antiques: The Mews: 1708 Market Center Blvd.; Dallas, Texas 75207; 214/443-9999

◀ Full size pattern for stenciled projects on pages 34-35 and 94.

Index

gardenstyle
projects